SALT IN THE
WOUND

A collection of literature inspired by the real stories submitted by women in my community, social media and beyond.

Resources to support:

Women's Aid – www.womensaid.org.uk

Action Aid – www.actionaid.org.uk

Malaika – www.malaika.org

Women for Afghan Women – www.womenforafghanwomen.org

Women for Women International – www.womenforwomen.org.uk

All royalties and sales from this book will be donated between the above charities.

ONE

72,

50,

46,

20.

72 years young,

50 years in wedded bliss,

46 men convicted,

20 year sentence.

83,

20,000,

4,

3.

83 men invited,

20,000 images found,

4 diseases contracted,

3 years for the defendant.

M'endors Pas

mendorspas.org

TWO

She ran when the sky split open,

when the earth spat out bones,

when men with guns carved history into her skin.

She ran because staying meant death,

but leaving meant something slower.

She sold her gold for passage,

her name for silence,

her body for mercy.

No one carries a woman through war—

she carries herself,

through borders that do not want her,

through hands that take more than they give.

She sleeps in rooms that smell of strangers,

mouths prayers to gods who have stopped listening.

Somewhere, a daughter still calls her name in the dark.

Somewhere, a past she cannot return to

rots under the weight of men's decisions.

But she is still here.

Still standing.

Still dangerous.

Because a woman who has survived hell

knows she can burn and not disappear.

THREE

He says he loves her with fists and silence,

with doors slammed shut, with nights that bleed.

She wears his rage like a second skin,

purple blooming where love should be.

She learns to measure storms in footsteps,

to read the weather in his breath.

A wrong word, a glance too long—

and she is the lightning rod again.

She paints on smiles in shades of survival,

hides bruises beneath long sleeves and lies.

"It's not so bad," she tells the mirror,

as shattered glass winks back in reply.

FOUR

They take her words first.

Not all at once,

No, that would be too obvious,

 They pluck them like petals from a flower, one by one,

You're too loud, too angry, too much,

 She learns to speak in softer tones, in whispers that do not unsettle.

Then they take her name,

Folding it neatly into the shadow of a man's,

She becomes his wife, their daughter, someone's mother,

Never just herself.

They take her stories next,

Call them exaggerations, call them hysteria

Call them nothing at all,

It didn't happen like that,

You're remembering wrong.

At last, they take her silence and call it peace.

But inside her,

Words still pulse like trapped birds against her rib,

She is waiting,

Not for permission,

No, she is done with that.

She is waiting for the moment they forget to keep their hands over her mouth.

And then, she will set the world on fire.

FIVE

His hands drip with gold and blood,

But only one of them is called a stain.

He sits high,

above the world,

his power unquestioned.

She stands below,

the weight of his decisions crushing her
shoulders.

She kneels,

as expected,

as required.

But deep inside,

she is measuring the distance between her
silence and his throat.

All kings fall eventually.

The best ones never see it coming.

SIX

They never said it outright,

but she learned it young:

A woman who is quiet is respected.

A woman who is loud is ruined.

She sits in meetings where men talk over her,

laugh at her ideas,

then repeat them as their own.

She watches how they smile at girls,

 all soft voices and small hands,

and call them "proper."

She wonders what they call a woman who doesn't give a damn anymore.

She thinks she'll find out soon.

SEVEN

He tells her he earned this power.

That he worked harder,

fought smarter,

played the game better.

That she should be grateful to live in a world shaped by men like him.

She wonders if he would still think so,

if the world shaped by men like him didn't have so many dead women in it.

EIGHT

She told the truth.

They called it a lie.

She showed them proof.

They called it a mistake.

She screamed.

They called her hysterical.

She stopped speaking altogether.

Finally, they called her a good woman.

NINE

They called them witches for knowing too much,

speaking too much,

wanting too much.

The truth?

They were only women who refused to be burned.

And those women never truly die.

TEN

She decorates the home he owns,

raises the children he named,

sleeps in the bed he chose.

And yet, when he turns cruel,

 when he turns cold,

it is her who should have tried harder.

ELEVEN

She learned early,

 that walking alone at night is reckless.

 That rejecting a man is dangerous.

That wearing the wrong thing is an invitation.

She wonders if they ever teach boys the same lessons.

TWELVE

They tell her her voice matters.

They send her to the polls with promises of change,

with hope dressed in blue and red.

But when she casts her ballot,

when she dares to demand the things they promised her,

they call her naïve.

They call her ungrateful.

They tell her that progress takes time,

they always say that.

They've been saying it for decades.

And when the men in power,

make deals behind closed doors,

when laws are passed that will never touch their children,

they call it politics.

They say she doesn't understand.

They say she's too emotional.

But she knows.

She knows that her voice,

was never meant to be heard.

She knows her body,

was never meant to be hers alone.

She knows the power,

has always been in their hands.

And so, she waits.

Not for permission.

Not for change.

But for the moment when the world finally listens.

THIRTEEN

She cries,

and they call her dramatic.

 She raises her voice,

 and they call her mad.

She fights back,

and they call her dangerous.

Funny how men fear a woman who feels too much.

Almost as much as they fear one who feels nothing at all.

FOURTEEN

Once, she was soft.

She swallowed apologies that were never spoken.

She shrank to make others comfortable.

But one day,

something in her snapped.

She stopped saying sorry.

Stopped explaining.

Stopped waiting for permission.

And suddenly, they called her cruel.

FIFTEEN

He doesn't need to wrap his hands,

around her neck to make her choke.

He does it with rules.

With expectations.

With the kind of love that tastes like control.

She can breathe,

but only when he lets her.

SIXTEEN

She saw something she wasn't supposed to.

Heard a conversation meant for men's ears only.

Knew a truth that could set the world on fire.

So they called her crazy.

Because it's easier to erase a woman's credibility,

than to erase the evidence.

SEVENTEEN

For him,

power is a birthright.

For her, it's a battle.

He steps into the room and is trusted.

She steps in and must prove she belongs.

He is strong.

She is aggressive.

He is decisive.

She is difficult.

He is a leader.

She is a bitch.

EIGHTEEN

They dressed it up for her.

Called it love.

Called it protection.

Called it tradition.

They built the bars from expectations,

and wrapped them in gold.

They handed her the key,

and told her freedom was hers anytime she wanted.

And yet,

somehow,

the door never opened.

NINETEEN

She carries her mother's warnings.

Her grandmother's grief.

She carries keys between her fingers at night,

 like tiny weapons.

She carries the weight of every woman before her,

who never got to walk away.

TWENTY

They call her bitter.

Call her angry.

Call her impossible.

She doesn't mind.

Because while they waste their breath naming her,

she is busy writing her own story.

TWENTY ONE

They told her she was beautiful.

Then they told her to cover up.

To smile more.

To not be so vain.

To not let herself go.

They made her wear her beauty like a weapon,

and a wound.

TWENTY TWO

They said she was foolish to leave.

That it wasn't that bad.

That women before her endured worse.

But the first breath she took as a free woman,

tasted like something she had never known before.

She decided she would rather be foolish,

than dead.

TWENTY THREE

They call her difficult.

Call her cold.

Call her heartless.

They don't see the ghosts behind her eyes.

The women who came before her.

The ones who were too kind.

Too soft.

Too trusting.

She carries their lessons like armour.

TWENTY FOUR

Don't be too loud.

Don't be too quiet.

Don't be too pretty.

Don't be too plain.

Don't make him mad.

Don't make him bored.

Don't make him think you don't need him.

She plays the game because she has to.

But one day, she will rewrite the rules.

TWENTY FIVE

They tried to silence her.

They called her names,

made her small,

turned her words to dust.

But they forgot something.

A woman who has tasted her own power,

will never kneel again.

Twenty Six

He calls her his queen in the dark,

 his whore in the light.

He takes her body,

then her name,

then her voice.

He signs laws,

 with the same hands that have choked the breath,

 from women just like her.

And when he's done,

he straightens his tie,

cleans his hands,

and speaks of morality.

TWENTY SEVEN

She was eight when they held her down.

Her mother whispered that it was tradition.

Her aunt held her wrists.

The old woman with the knife said nothing at all.

Afterward,

they called her pure.

They called her clean.

They called her worthy of a man.

She bled for weeks.

She never spoke of it again.

TWENTY EIGHT

He builds nations with stolen hands.

He writes laws to protect his own sins.

He names wars after freedom,

after justice,

after peace.

But at night,

when his soldiers burn villages,

and take girls who still have baby teeth,

he sleeps soundly.

TWENTY NINE

They paid her to forget.

Paid her to unsee the hands,

the bruises,

the ripped lace.

Paid her to turn her pain into a receipt.

And in the morning,

they passed laws about family values.

THIRTY

Men wrote the rules.

Men built the walls.

Men decided who was human,

and who was property.

And when she screamed,

they asked for proof.

When she bled,

they asked if she had deserved it.

When she died,

they called it a tragedy.

And when another girl took her place,

they called it fate.

THIRTY ONE

She was raised in marble halls,

dressed in silk,

fed on lies.

She thought her father was a king,

not a killer.

She thought the streets were quiet,

because the people were happy.

Then one night,

she found the bodies.

And the next morning,

her father's men made sure she never spoke of them.

Thirty Two

She came in for help.

He told her she was broken.

He said women like her were too wild,

too disobedient,

too much.

So he cut.

He carved.

He took pieces of her away,

until she was small enough to be controlled.

Then he wrote in his notes:

Cured.

THIRTY THREE

She learned how to obey.

How to swallow rage like a bitter pill.

She learned how to dress,

so he wouldn't look elsewhere,

but never so well,

that he thought she was trying too hard.

She learned how to please him,

even when it hurt.

And when she learned how to stop loving him,

they called her a disgrace.

THIRTY FOUR

She stood before them,

armed with facts,

with fire,

with truth.

They called her emotional.

They let her speak,

then ignored her completely.

Then they signed laws about her body,

her rights,

her life,

without ever looking her in the eye.

Thirty Five

They told women to be patient.

To wait their turn.

To use their voices,

but never too loudly.

Then the women set the world on fire.

And suddenly,

they weren't called women anymore.

They were called monsters.

THIRTY SIX

She kissed a boy.

Her brother slit her throat.

She laughed in a cafe.

Her father poured gasoline over her body.

She spoke to a man who was not her husband.

Her family called it justice.

They buried her in a shallow grave.

The next day,

they ate breakfast like nothing had happened.

THIRTY SEVEN

They made Him a man.

Gave Him anger,

gave Him fists,

gave Him laws that favored only themselves.

Then they told her to bow.

To kneel.

To thank Him for her suffering.

And when she dared to ask why,

they called it blasphemy.

THIRTY EIGHT

She stood beside him,

as he preached about virtue.

She smiled as he shook hands with men,

 who whispered about her body behind his back.

She stayed silent,

when his belt cracked against her ribs.

Then one day,

she woke up and set his house on fire.

THIRTY NINE

They ran from war,

from famine,

from men who saw them as prey.

They thought the camps would be safe.

But the guards had hands just like the soldiers.

And at night,

when no one was watching,

the girls learned there was nowhere left to run.

FORTY

She told them she wasn't crazy.

That the bruises were real.

That the nightmares had teeth.

That she could still hear the screams.

They nodded,

wrote down psychotic episode,

and handed her a pill.

She stopped screaming.

They called it progress.

FORTY ONE

The boys laughed.

The teacher looked away.

The girls shrank smaller in their seats.

She raised her hand, called it what it was.

Assault.

Violence.

Hate.

They told her she was overreacting.

And when the boys did worse,

when the laughter turned into scars,

they asked her why she hadn't spoken up sooner.

FORTY TWO

They bombed clinics,

and called it morality.

They banned contraception

and called it protection.

They forced birth

and called it life.

And when women died screaming,

bleeding,

choking on their own blood,

they called it God's will.

FORTY THREE

She was six,

when they told her she was unclean.

Seven,

when they held her down.

Eight,

when she stopped feeling anything at all.

And when she turned twelve,

and a man three times her age took her as his wife,

they called her blessed.

FORTY FOUR

They elect men who hate them.

They pass laws that crush them.

They let them die,

at the hands of their husbands

and call it unfortunate.

And still,

they wonder why the women are angry.

FORTY FIVE

They buried her sisters.

They silenced her mother.

They broke her bones and still,

she would not kneel.

And when they asked her why,

 she refused to die quietly,

she simply smiled and said:

Because you haven't learned how to kill me yet.

FORTY SIX

46 men convicted.

Printed in Great Britain
by Amazon